lover

lover

Gloria Herdt

Copyright 2026 Gloria Herdt
All rights reserved, including the right to reproduce this book or portions thereof in any form whatsoever without written permission, except in the case of reprints in the context of reviews. No part of this book may be used or reproduced in any manner for the purpose of training artificial intelligence technologies or systems.

First printed edition: February 2026
Cover & interior line art by: Travis Herdt
Printed in the United States
Bear & Fox Publishing
Paperback ISBN: 979-8-9941407-0-3

*For my biggest crush,
the one who almost got away,
my lover, my best friend, my husband,
the most brilliant creative I've ever known,*

*who knew our first trip to Las Vegas
would spark an entire poetry collection ...*

I've always been in love
with beautiful things.

The diamond ring I yearned to see on my finger.
Love that could last the test of time, I'd be so cozy
wrapped up in adoration. A cashmere sweater in the richest
emerald green. I always wanted my eyes to be that shade,
but they were lighter, more golden to match my hair
after I'd spent a day in the sun. Sugar crystal sand
warm under my feet. A cleansing sweep of the tide.
Ocean waves curling their fingers around seashells
and a silver dollar I found once. Entirely whole. A miracle
to hold in my hands as the sun settled—fully bloomed
into pink and purple hues.
I sent a wish out into the sea
that one day I'd see myself as a beautiful thing.

We were wild once.

You and I

roaming darkened alleyways,
catching late night trains
to unmarked places.
Our favorite space   that rocky ledge.
The city glittered at our feet.

I'll never forget that one night,
starlight reflecting in your eyes
when you pointed to the glowing skyline
and told me the city was mine.

But the world tamed us,
whipped the dreams right out of our chests,
told us it was normal to be chained to an hourglass
drained of every last grain of sand. We wore collars
of unworthiness pulled tight by childhood wounds
and fears of never living up to expectations.
Pressure to perform suffocating.

Now, you look at me, eyes bloodshot and listless,
the weariness of every day breaking us slowly.

And I know
it's my turn to shine the light for us,
to catch all the stars in my hand
and revive the dreams we once had.

I won't let our spark die inside this cage.

My love, please trust me when I say,
we can be wild again.

Some of life's greatest adventures
start with a simple request:

will you come with me?

I take my first steps off the plane.
My heart leaps ahead.

I am stuffed with jitters and healthy snacks
that I packed for the five-hour journey,
yet I am already imagining a decadent meal
at a glitzy restaurant. Champagne glasses clinking around
the room in unified celebration.

We are in Vegas.

I exit the dimly lit tunnel, blinking wildly, my eyes adjusting to
all the color and light. Bright yellow, red, and orange glow
from a circle of slot machines.

Gemstones. Gold coins. Dollar bills dance
on oversized screens.

The sound of winning and losing is all around me.
When I leave this city, which side will I be on?

There are empty seats, but I don't feel the urge to play.
I've never gambled before — at least not in this way.

      I've only ever put my heart on the table.

We got married on a freezing cold day in November.
I didn't care that my lips were blue like your eyes
an ocean before me. I'd plummet gladly.

Your gaze never left my face even as the harsh New England
wind whipped off the sea, scraping your beard, setting all the
delicate curls in my hair free.

We got married in the wild.
Our backs to scrubby brush and jagged rocks with marbled
veins of white. My dress a simple sheath of silky fabric.
No protection from the elements. But you gave me the last bit
of warmth in your hands as you pulled me closer, threaded us
together, our vows trailing behind us
as we danced our first married dance among the pines.

No music. My veil left behind.

None of it mattered.

We got married with starlight in our eyes
even though it wasn't dark, even though the sun didn't shine
for us that day. It was misty and damp and overcast.

Yet our hearts were on fire for each other
and in that final hour, even nature couldn't deny us
a beautiful gift. A dark ocean expanse lit by a radiant
golden sunset.

I swore I'd never visit Las Vegas.

A city that advertised *sin* in its well-worn name
was not a place for a devout good girl.

Five years ago, I would've looked down on myself,
pronounced I'd fallen from grace.

Now, thirty-two stories above the Vegas Strip,
I can't stop my smile from breaking every hardened line
on my face, glowing through the cracks,
bouncing off the hotel glass,
reflecting my golden light back.

I had no idea how fun it would be
to rise above my own limiting beliefs.

Every city has a heart beat
a pulse that sets the tempo beneath my feet.
An invitation to sync my nervous system.

Colorful fiber wires imbedded in the sidewalks,
emitting signals I can decode
if I hone my attention.

In New York it was red hot,
       didn't stop pushing me forward,
       a heavy handedness that made me want more.

Boston was cool blues and greens,
       swirling together, charming me
       into achieving my dreams.

But Vegas is different.
       A kaleidoscope of neon light
       playing with my mind, asking
           who do you want to be here?

I've never been one of those women
who can look sexy when they part their lips,
like they're waiting to tell you the most scandalous secret.

I look like I've fallen asleep, mouth open,
my crooked teeth jutting forward like they're warding off
intruders.

I've tried a hundred times to make a sexy face
in the bathroom mirror,
in the tiny camera on my phone,
no matter how small the pixels,
I can still see my front teeth in the narrow crease that's
supposed to be a black hole—a portal
one could imagine slipping *something* into.

I ruin that illusion.
My teeth competing for the front seat.

When I was twenty-five, my dentist told me,
you'd be so beautiful if you had a straight smile.
He said he could fix it.
Make me beautiful.

I never went back.
Even then, I was tired of picking at myself
with a scalpel made of other people's desires.

Glossy hotel floors
polished to the highest shine,
golden elevators, glass tables,
pristine floor to ceiling windows,
this place is a city of mirrors.

What does it mean to be *sexy?*

Is it a feeling? Or an image?
A circular target to hit
with the sway of my hips
or the way I move my lips,
and once I do,
I'll feel a different relationship to my body

                        and the world will finally notice

wanting me so much more
than I ever wanted it.

The patio is bustling,
couples and large groups sipping on cocktails,
bubbling up laughter.

I'm seated at a granite and iron table.
A table for one.
I sip sparkling water, gaze drifting
between my diamond wedding ring and the Bellagio fountains
dancing across the street.

This was supposed to be my husband's work trip.
But I've turned it into a sexy vacation
like in the movies,
except there's cigarette smoke stuck in my nose
and a drunken man spitting too close.

A sparrow perches on a curved tree branch above my head
and sings to me—cutting through the noise.

There's always beauty if I'm willing to see it.

Exquisite deviled eggs topped with caviar. Art on a plate.
I wine and dine myself. The sky blushes for the last time today.

More people flock to the sidewalk, dressed in everything from
backyard casual to disco glam, holding hourglass Daiqueri cups
and lovers' hands.

I feel a flutter in my chest.
Will I have mind-blowing sex in Vegas?

I left the hotel suite so confident,
my turquoise mini dress showing off every inch of me.
Hiding a little secret:
I'm wearing nothing underneath.

I devour a plate of roast chicken and potatoes
with sensual focus, humming a chord of deliciousness,
then pay the bill, join the rush on The Strip.

Out of thousands of people in this crowd,
I'd say my odds for a good time are high.

What if it were easy for me to walk down the street
holding my own hand?

I'd meet the eyes of strangers with such confidence
they'd swear I was someone important,
someone deserving of one hundred long-stemmed roses,
pert and red, tucked under them
a little note that said,

> *You've always been worth it.*

Would I believe it
if it were in my tiny, messy handwriting?
My fingers feverishly scribbling
on a thick square of gold cardstock,
twenty-four-carat
soft and delicate,
I've always wanted to be that precious.

Vegas is a city with no expectations, no limitations,
where you can be *anyone, anything,*
so, I've come to be my sexiest self—the one who
shows off her shape and catches the eye
even with a belly full of nourishment.

There are women in the streets
dressed in bejeweled burlesque costumes,
tiny thongs so revealing.
They laugh with each other,
butts jiggling as they pass—firm, round, dimpled,
slightly sagging and it doesn't matter.
They invite people to take photos with them,
a *permanent* document of their form.

Behind them, I strut down The Strip
in my tight blue dress, knowing full well
I am *not* a perfect straight line.
There are parts of me pulling the cotton fabric—
some in places I like, others I mind
and I remember all those times
I ate baby carrots for every meal,
and lived in the gym instead of my own body,
trapped in a cage of ideals
I'd constructed out of magazines and movies.

But Las Vegas is a place where I get to bring
all of me— both the one who judges
and the one who's already been set *free.*

I stand in line
to see the Vegas skyline from the top of the Eiffel Tower.
Think of you
at your company dinner
that feels a thousand miles away.
Decide to go back to our hotel,
the view of you is clearer there. Climb into bed,
dream we're already together.

I loved you before you ever let me in.
Waited years for you to open up
just a little bit.
I snuck in
through the crack in your foundation.
Squeezing my insides
to fit into
the smallest
spaces.
Barely breathing
my footsteps so light
you couldn't hear me coming.

Some days it hurt to hear the echo of my heart
in all that empty space—

knowing I had to keep my distance,

watching the way you touched the strings of your guitar,
your mouth moving with the notes. And I wanted *so badly*
to be the music you kept coming back to.

The desperation to touch you burning the edges of all
the pages I was writing. My hand scribbling till it ached.

But I couldn't stop writing our names together,
couldn't stop writing our story of forever.

Let me
curl up
beside you,
feel the way
air
travels
down
your spine.
I've always wanted
to be this close.
The rhythm
of your heart
syncing with mine.

I don't think I *really knew* what it meant to be married,

that my husband and I would have to
take our egos off the shelf,

shatter them all over the floor
so we could study the pieces that made us whole.

In this mess of honesty,
we'd have a better shot at *forever.*

My heart rate slows inside the *Bodies* exhibit.
The air in the room cools my skin, overheated from walking
through New York City, past the sunlit Statue of Liberty, and
great pyramids guarded by stone pharaohs—designed
beautifully to mimic the real thing. Yet my visceral wonder
waits for human anatomy.

I'm surrounded by bones and organs.
All of it inside of me. The darker space lit by tiny spotlights.
Cardiac, respiratory, reproductive, and nervous systems
all shining like fine jewelry in glass cases.

I study the valves and vessels of a heart,
trying to understand how it all works.

There's a sign with all the information I need,
yet even as I read   nothing   is   sticking.

The heart tissue is hardened and yellow,
a side effect of preservation.

I used to know the inner workings of the aorta
and how many beats per minute a healthy heart makes,
but all my years of worrying and ignoring my body's signals
erased the information from my brain,
making space for more important things
like how it feels to survive heartbreak.

I can't tear my eyes away from this heart on its back
in peaceful surrender or defeat?   I'll never know.

My phone stays listless in my pocket. A weight
I don't reach for in this weightless moment.

I need to feel my heart beating in my chest,
press down with my hand,
searching for buried treasure.

There it is.

The pulse beneath my palm. Smooth and steady.
I breathe.

I am alive.

I am alive.

I am alive.

It's magic,
a mirror trick that plays with my mind.

I am looking at a heart and feeling a heart
all at the same time.

This one calcified and frozen. Mine rich with blood,
wet and throbbing.

Tears spring to my eyes.
It's all so real. *My insides on the outside.*

And in the darkened room with no one around,
> I bow my head and cry.

A little white sign catches my eye in the *Bodies* exhibit:
if all of the muscles in your body worked together,
you could lift more than 10 tons.

I could lift a massive elephant if only I wasn't so busy
carrying around all my feelings of not-enough-ness.

Not pretty enough.
Not thin enough.
Not toned enough.
Not strong enough.
Not enough ass, not enough breasts.
Not enough confidence.
Not good enough.
Not cool enough.
Not enough sparkle or shine.
Not enough volume to my hair or my voice or heaven-forbid
too much.

I've been too busy stretching my limbs in different directions,
seeking favor and attention in everyone—anyone who isn't me.
My face constantly changing to meet the demands
of what I think you want to see.

You were the mirror I stood in front of
to decide how I felt about myself
and I realize now
what a big mistake that was
to search your eyes
for my worth
on a bad day
when you were stressed about money
or angry that the dryer broke again.

I used to think the room got cold because I walked in,

my hair still wet from showering off
shame growing thicker by the day
under my skin.
Stomach and thighs jiggled in cotton pajama pants.
You had rock hard abs from working out every day.

I had to look the other way whenever I saw my reflection,
the tight body you said you loved
replaced with something more relaxed.

I was a knotted ball of nerves inside,

wondering ...

if you'd choose me on any given night,
obsessed with *you* determining *my beauty*.

But your mouth didn't move,
jaw stayed clenched.

I read the silence.

Rejection.

Went to bed dreaming
of compliments flying from your lips,
fluttering kisses,
so, I'd know for sure
I was still the one you wanted.

But now I see the truth. The real mirror of my worth.

> *I* have to want *me* first.

I want to love this body before it's too late
before my knees are weak
and I can't rise from my seat easily.
Before the last sunrise in me goes down.

I want to love this body before my vibrancy fades,
mind dims, the shades of thought blending together
until I can't articulate the way I feel anymore.

I want to love this body
before it's the ideal shape or weight.

    I want to love my body now.

Somewhere along the way,
I realized that abandoning myself,
my needs,
my dreams,
my desires,
was never the way to get closer to someone else.
It would just leave me feeling
incomplete inside of love.

I wasn't looking for a lover in Vegas.
Just wanted a break from routine,
out of the ordinary
to make me believe I was still a woman in her prime,
hotter than the steak I served for Friday night dinner,
eager to sizzle all the way down to my tender red center,
let my juices run onto the plate
have someone lick their lips and say, *damn!*

My lover found me. In a restaurant of all places.
His sensuous gaze only ever leaving my face
to travel to my breasts and maybe in this day and age
I'm supposed to mind, but I'm already staring
at his well-defined biceps riding out from under his shirt.

I'd undo every button with my teeth
if I thought I could do it without giggling,
my self-consciousness too cumbersome
for me to be that clever.

I'm out of practice. He doesn't mind.

I blush, yet we've been lost in the mundane
for the same amount of time.

There's a glint of surprise in his eyes
when he tells me I'm beautiful,

Is this *whole-body-tingling* desire new for him too?

The candle on the table casts shadows over our hands.
Light catches on my wedding band.

We trace each other's palms like we're reading the future.

Our fingertips map all the ways
we'll touch each other when dinner is over.

I've always wanted to be touched like this,
made to feel time was resting by my side,
your lips poised over mine,
ready to tell me all your secret desires.

What makes you come alive?

I want to feel the moment when the blood rushes
to the surface of your skin.

My heart's already on fire, a slow burn that started
before I can remember. Let's dive into ecstasy together,
forget the people we were before.

I seek out your hand
in the middle of the night,
my fingers searching for yours
under the covers,
like long lost lovers.
Can't get enough
of each other.

How many new ways are there
for us to feel closer?

You're still dreaming

yet somehow
you know what I need.

Our hands hold tight.

first thought:
I want you
still in bed
cozy under the sheets
throbbing
heartbeat
spreads down my body
warm, haziness between
sleep and waking
mind not yet online
primal desire turns on
swelling pleasure
merging hard and soft places
the first honest sounds from our voices.
We come fully awake, fully alive
just as the sun rises.

Everyone keeps telling me how lucky I am
to have come to Vegas this week.

The temperatures tempered from recent rain,
a cleansing for the city.

A comfortable mid-eighty-degree day,
perfect for a leisurely stroll among well-fed greenery.

The sun strokes my face.
We have had our rest.
        Our luck is only just rising.

We rendezvous in Paris
Peruse the shops of Venice.
Gaze at fine art in Rome.
    And still, I'd say my favorite place
    is under the hotel sheets with you.

Oh, how I want to jump into one of these fountains!
Submerge myself in the crystal-clear water.
I wouldn't have to be afraid of bright blue pulling me under.

I'd float effortlessly on my back. Energetic sprays
ever so refreshing. Showered by opulent overflowing basins,
protected by horse-mermaid sculptures and the feminine body
with wings.

Oh, the delicious fizzy joy I feel even now, imagining
splashing around in all that flawless beauty.

Your body looks like a Greek god,
a Roman statue,
every muscle of you
hard as marble
much hotter than the sculptures in Caesar's Palace
we braved the late-morning heat to view.

I laughed
when I said *they didn't do you justice.*

Now, I can't catch my breath,
tracing every ripple where your strength lives.

What would we say
if someone cast us in clay
and we got the chance to see ourselves in this position?

If I wasn't afraid of getting arrested,
I'd have you on the casino floor,
screaming your name between gulping wet breaths
of ecstasy so that everyone would know
the primal sound of winning.

I thought Nevada was going to be a barren desert.
Nothing more than scorching heat and dust.
But the winding drive through the Red Rock Canyon
reveals green scrubby brush and yellow flowers
stretching their necks toward the sun.

I get out of the rented Jeep,
almost lose my footing.
I'm not used to being so far from the ground.

The air is rich with a fragrance I can't define.
Natural, fresh, a hint of something fertile.
This must be the signature scent of the desert.

Only the strongest will survive here.

We walk a narrow path between twisted trees.
I can't believe how much green covers my vision.
Tiny purple and orange flowers sprout up everywhere,
the first act before reddish gray mountains appear like giants
rising, their heads touching the cornflower blue sky.

I am so small here.
Yet I feel as vast as the rocky expanse stretched out
like an everchanging canvas.

The plants have adapted to retain the rain.
In small pockets water pools, giving life to a verdant canopy.
A secret paradise.

Here, time doesn't mean as much.
There's no rush.

It's easier for us
to give in to the heated desire that's always *waiting*
below our horizon line.

A bride and groom take pictures
in front of The Bellagio fountains.
Tourists stare at their newlywed bliss.
Surrounded by opulent columns and exotic flowers
so colorful they look fake.

Is their love real?

People say marry your best friend,
but my husband and I didn't start out like that.
It's just the story we tell people because it sounds better.

Our friendship grew out of lust and longing
much later. We stripped each other down,
teased out all our threads of connection
to see if we were still lovable underneath.

I find an empty lounge chair by the pool.
Strip down to my pink bathing suit.
I almost didn't buy it. Thinking it was too tiny.
The ruffles on the bottom too flirty
for my thirty-eight-year-old body.

I sit at the edge of the shallow-end,
the lower half of my leg submerged in water only a couple
degrees cooler than the air temperature. I savor it anyway,
shocked by the impulse to take a bathing suit selfie.

I hold my phone up high to get a flattering angle
from lips to thighs, just the way my lover likes to see me.

Heat prickles my skin.
I hold my breath.
Hesitate before pressing send.

I remember when my belly never wrinkled,
when I was a crisp twenty, laying by a pool in Miami.
I was toned and tanned in my black and white floral bikini,
not an inch of me out of place no matter my position.

For years—in secret—I treasured that glossy photo
like a diamond ring.

But what did it cost me to be that thin?

Countless hours in the gym,
counting calories like my life depended on it,
more supplements and fat burners than actual food,
and in the end, what was my prize?

A double-zero dress size.

I claim my moment under the summer sun,
send the sexy picture to my lover.

Maybe there's too much *realness* for his taste,
but why does more of me have to be a bad thing?

The hotel pool is bursting with bodies of all sizes.
I jump in, refreshed by their cool confidence.

A woman pulls me into a conversation,
tells me how good I look in my bikini.

I admit when I turned thirty, I started wearing one-pieces
because I thought I was too old, should cover up my body.

She says, *that's crazy!* I have a killer figure. She's got the kind of
breasts I've always coveted—round and full—bursting
from her tiny triangle top.

And I just keep thinking that in Vegas,
there's no such thing as too much.

People said we should go see a show,
but when I slipped into that slinky black dress
your jaw fell to the floor and I thought
it'd be more fun to make one of our own.

Touch me till I burn so bright the stars are jealous.

In the hotel suite, I stand in front of a full-length mirror,
still flushed from orgasmic heat.
White sheets rumpled on the bed behind me.

I study each wrinkle and dimple on my body.
The lumpy places where I've lost my elasticity.
There's a flash of wanting,
a familiar hunger to shrink down to the floor,
grieve my younger, tighter self
yet I don't abandon my reflection,
the corner of my lip curls in scintillating satisfaction.

It's much more fun to be this loose.

I take a full breath and watch my belly grow,
feel the air reach all the places it couldn't years before—
my back, my sides,
stretching down into places that still tingle
with wet pleasure.

I stand up taller,
each breath getting longer as my gaze drifts
to the curves at my waist,
the scars on my wrist,
a skin tag on my upper thighs. Strong thighs
that have carried me across so many cities.

Sunlight beams through the windows,
matching my insides. I place my hands on the soft place
beneath my belly button, make a little heart with my hands.

I am proud of the woman I am becoming.

The one who can stand in front of a mirror,
see her beauty clearer,
and not wish she were someone else.

I don't wear lipstick
yet I still leave a mark when we kiss
every wish I've ever had for us
alive on my lips
blooms like a blush
brushed on bare cheeks
my face dusted with gold from our fourteen-year lust.

    I'm pretty sure glamour never looked this good.

I touch myself
till I forget who I'm supposed to be
till I'm liquid spilling all over the floor
unable to be cleaned up
the kind of mess that becomes part of the foundation
like it was always meant to be there
that one day will take my breath away
when I step back and see the mark I left on this place.

1. A slinky black dress
2. Supple leather of a designer purse
3. Golden sandals that shine in the sun
4. My skin tan and warm, caressed by a fresh breeze
5. Bright green of palm trees
6. A bold blue sky
7. The sparkle of my diamond ring

Tonight, I decide my smile makes the list
of beautiful, treasured things.

hot skin
wet lips
a hint of citrus and rum on your tongue.
I was drunk on you before we even got to the restaurant.

I think at one point
        my heart was beating so fast
                it exploded out of my chest,

made a rainbow-mess on the Vegas sidewalk.

        People applauded.

Afterall, this is a city that likes their pleasure

        out in the open.

The restaurant isn't what we expected.
Performers in sequined dresses and suits
Conga past our table. I wiggle my hips in my seat,
roll my shoulders to the drumming beat
and laugh at my own giddiness—
my willingness
to let myself have the moment
instead of watching from the outside.

My lover sits across from me,
but I've turned my body toward the party.
I'm not putting on a show for him.
I am dancing for myself.

The performers cheer me on
and after it's all over,
my lover takes my hand and says,

I love this side of you.

Back home my husband and I got a king-sized bed
so we could have more space.

Here, you and I meet in the middle.
Our bodies exchanging heat.

I reach for what I want most
before either of us have left the drowsiness of sleep.

In Vegas, everything is on the table.

We haven't made it to one of the hotel buffet's yet,
but I've heard the plates are overflowing with delicious
temptations.

I'm used to making every single breakfast.
Responsibility calling before my eyes fully open.

Now, you look like you want to devour me.
My longing feeds the air.

Pulsing. Heart. Breath. Pulsing between legs, lips
spread to match your devilish smile.

    I love that I'm the only thing on the menu.

Your kisses are satin on my lips,
fingers tracing hips
makes my blood turn to liquid gold.
I shimmer. I sparkle
in the light of your gaze.
The sounds we make are different here.
Our breathing heavy,
covering the hotel room in a dreamy haze.
Maybe it's better
we lose the outline of each other.

What do you think?
You ask me as we roam the Bellagio's art gallery.

I think it's funny
how you always want to know what I see
when you're the one who majored in art history,
anatomy, and fine art.

The painting we're standing in front of
reminds me of eyelashes batting all over the canvas.

Your take is that the artist feels incomplete,
pulled in too many directions,
frazzled thoughts leading to nowhere.

I lean in to read the little white sign with the artist's intent,
laugh out loud because you're right. *Again.*
I say *you're brilliant.* You shrug and pull me closer.

I still see hundreds of eyelashes, but now they're waving
goodbye as we disappear around the corner toward another
painting.

You tell me, *I love to hear all your thoughts*,
and I love that we're headed in the same direction.

There are escalators everywhere in Vegas.
Steep and long, short and fast. One feeding into another.
I feel like I'm falling—
that was always my fear. That I'd lose my footing,
end up shredded to bloody bits in the crooked teeth
of a moving machine.

First step on, last step off, I always hold my breath.
It's no different on this spiraling escalator
rising like a tower inside Caesar's Palace.

My husband stays one step ahead. I never like it
when someone's behind me, rushing me, pushing me forward.
I will not fall! I will not plummet to my death on a moving staircase!

Light touches my face.
We are almost to the top.
Glass windows, curved archways,
and white columns with ornate filigree
make it feel like we're climbing into heaven.
If only the vibration under my feet wasn't so scary,
I'd lose myself in this moment. Instead, I'm focused
on getting closer to the end.

My husband reaches out for my hand and I take it,
my lungs high up in my chest, the pressure building
as I take my last step.

Hah, sweet release! I am safe on solid ground, marble tiles
smooth under sandaled feet.

The art gallery is straight ahead. We finally found it
and from the look on my husband's face—the purest,
most joyous smile I've seen in a while—I'd say the view
was well worth the climb.

I love that feeling
when you walk into a place and somehow
there's more space in your lungs
for deeper breaths
and your heart whispers,
this is my kind of beautiful.

The gallery is cozy.
Awash in vivid color and bronze sculptures.

I'm surrounded by dreamy paintings. A city brownstone
opens up like a book. Some of the windows lit
with a soft glow, others dark, windows closed.
My mind spins with all the possible stories,
secrets kept inside.

There's a painting of a caterpillar admiring itself in the mirror,
pondering what to wear—a cozy chrysalis suit or a pair of
intricate, colorful wings? Giant butterflies become sails
of a regal ship headed toward home. Another butterfly
in a sweet apple's core.

I am still
in front of a bronze sculpture—a woman with book pages
between her legs. Can't tear my eyes away. My passion for
beauty merging with creativity. Appetite wet from all the
delicious things I see and feel within me.

Lovers in a bedroom, suspended in the cosmos.
A shooting star outside.

I could stare at these paintings and sculptures for hours.
My head buzzing from wonder. These surreal worlds
perfect mirrors for the mess inside my head. All of it
suddenly making sense.

I've always said my favorite paintings were Monet's water lilies,
the impressionist-era softness the epitome of beauty.
But if I'm honest, I'm secretly in love with the work of the
surrealist.

I made a piece once in high school art class.
A colored pencil drawing of a tiger's head coming out of a
woman and a glass orb giving birth to a rose, and things were
sprouting from other things until I didn't know what the origin
of the thing was anymore.

Black and white tiles lined the floor—the last trace of logic and
reason. And I remember how much I loved letting go
of myself in the chaos.

Now, I'm on the verge of tears,
all my sensitivity breaking the surface.
My skin so tender. One touch and I'd burst wide open.
A new piece of art: *the woman who became a river overflowing.*

I turn to my husband, look him in the eyes, and tell him
for the very first time, *I love surrealism.*

I don't believe in guilty pleasures.
I believe in proud pleasures,
shouted from the rooftop
or quietly whispered
cozy under the covers.

Never waking with an alarm.
Dancing to an EDM song.
Putting on luscious, silky face cream like I'm a goddess.
Countless hours spent day-dreaming.
Reading for a whole day.
Art I make anyway, even if it's just for me.
Half a day streaming romance tv.
Devouring a third pumpkin cupcake
licking the last bit of frosting off the plate.

There's a giant LOVE sculpture in the Venetian hotel
made of red metal letters.

My husband asks if I want a picture. I don't really.
I think it's kind of cheesy, but I'm afraid
I'll wish for this moment when the trip is over.

Everyone else seems enamored by these simple, life-sized
letters. A revolving door of families and couples
striking a pose, arms outstretched to take another photo
for the group behind them.

And I can't help smiling,
a simple magic brewing in the hotel air
that's got me feeling lighter than the oxygen
they pump into casinos to keep you playing.

But there are no games here. No high rollers.
Just ordinary people loving on each other, choosing a letter
from the L-O-V-E to stand in front of or squeeze inside.
Smile at the camera, remember this feeling of being together.

When it's my turn, I throw my hands up to the sky.
I try to be as big as *LOVE*.

I didn't know if we'd make it here in time
to see the sparkling lights.
The way your smile changes with the sun,
I'd pay anything to see it rise forever.
Did I ever tell you how much *I love* your laugh?
The way your mouth gives way to the most glorious sound.
I've never heard an angel sing,
but I doubt they'd make me feel as safe.

On our wedding day, when I said, *you have my heart forever*

                                          I meant it.

Strong coffee.
Buttery, salty fried chicken
and fluffy waffles with bourbon maple syrup.
The table is tiny, music too loud
but we don't need to hear each other
to know what we're thinking:
this is delicious!
Sex this morning, now breakfast
savory and sweet
my tongue still remembers stroking you
and I wonder if you're thinking the same thing.

There isn't enough alcohol in the syrup to get us wasted,
yet we've got our drunk smiles on, and it makes me think of
the early days when I had to drink to loosen my lips enough
to tell you how I really felt.

Remember that night on Bowdoin Street in Boston?
My face flush from too many Jack and Cokes
and keeping my feelings too close to my chest.
I blurted out,
I really like you! so loud I startled the pigeons.
You laughed like you already knew.

I lean across the mess on my plate,
thousands of miles from where we started,
and shout over the music, *I love you!*

I'll never forget the way you took my hand
after we said our vows,
got pronounced as husband and wife.
You took me by surprise
when you smiled as if you were the happiest man alive.
Led me down the steep, rocky path
away from the open ocean
like suddenly there was nothing more important
than shielding me from the elements.
I felt you take on your new role
with such serious commitment. You held my hand
like I was precious—I guess I forgot about that. How you
made me feel not only desirable that day, but irreplaceable.

We wander around the MGM Grand,
watching people play slots, roulette, and black jack.
Neither of us are fired up to play.
Maybe it's because it's our last night here
and by morning,
I'll be dressed in routine and stress. You distant.

We walk hand-in-hand off the casino floor,
our fingertips seeking out any skin
that still needs to be touched.

With each gliding step toward the elevator bank,
the silk of my pants caresses my thighs
the same way I know you will
once the doors close.

The lights are dim at the end of the lobby.
I imagine you untying my top
before we reach the penthouse floor.

But you spin me around. Catch me off guard.
My pulse quickens to keep pace with my strides
as you guide me back to the golden glow.
Away from our room.

I want to see you win, you say
as if this is your only desire for tonight.
Your eyes are bright and aimed at me
with a grin on your face that makes me believe
I could actually win.

We hurry toward the roulette tables.
I pick one where everyone's laughing. A sure bet
I'll have fun.

You palm four crisp twenties into my hand.
I feel the rush of the game,
throw the money on the velvet table.

Before the chips come my way,
I smile at you—*my best friend, my lover, my husband*—
with everything I've got.

I still feel
the desert sun on my skin,
salty lips from our last meal.
I lean into you for one last kiss.
Let's take this feeling of Vegas home with us.

You emerge from your office.
I come out of the laundry room and I assume
you'll brush past me in the hallway. Like you used to—

But the air shifts
in my lungs,
around my arms.

You reach out to hold *me,*
pull me closer,
wrap me in the warmest hug.

You don't let go. You let me stay. A mountain of comfort.

Your chest rising and falling. Heartbeat under my ear.
The dryer whirring behind us, between us memories
of finding lovers in each other
in *Las Vegas*.

Return to love.
I think that's the secret to our marriage.
Return to love within myself
until I feel *my* wholeness, *my* worthiness
of love itself.

Return to love until I'm so full
I'm bursting with golden pink sparkling light
and you can't take your eyes off the shining love
you feel inside of me—it fills the space between us,
igniting our shared desire for closeness.

This is our marriage.

Both of us whole. Two pillars of love. Both of us complete.
Always returning to the source of *LOVE* whenever we need.

———— ‹‹ ———— ‹‹♥›› ———— ›› ————

Appreciation ♥

One of my favorite ways to feel the essence of love is appreciation!

Thank you, dear reader, for spending time in my world. For going on this poetic journey of loving exploration. Thank you for letting me relive this magical vacation. Thank you for feeling the depths of my love. I hope you remember, dear reader, you are always deserving of golden, glittering, whole-body-tingling *love*.

Extra hugs and kisses to my husband, Travis. When you asked me to go to Las Vegas for your work trip, I had no idea it was going to become a poetry collection, but I'm so damn glad it did! Thank you for the many (many) beautiful covers you made for *Lover*. You were so patient with me as I navigated art directing for the first time and making decisions for the look and feel of this collection, trying to get it just right. I'm so lucky to be married to you, to share breakfast with you every morning and open up our creative channel together with both realistic and completely wild ideas. Thank you for believing in me, for supporting my expansion, and reminding me (frequently) that I can do anything.

Thank you to my sister, Vicky, for gushing with me over the book covers that Travis made and watching our fur baby, Coorsy (aka Monkey, aka Mink) Thank you for taking such good care of him and giving him all the extra pets and outdoor adventures a dog that's as sassy as him could ask for. Because of your love and attention, I could relax on our trip (and leave the phone in my bag) knowing Coors was having the best time with you.

Thank you to my mom (aka Mam) for being the guiding light of love in my life. I believed in love from the moment I was born because of you. Thank you for listening to some of the early poem drafts. Your laughter and celebration meant the world to me.

Thank you to my writing buddy, Chris, for your grounded, intuitive guidance and unwavering willingness to call out anyone (including myself) who wants to shit on my parade. Thank you for comparing my poetry to Taylor Swift's songs (I'll forever be blushing from that one). Your support lovingly pushed me to publish even when I was afraid that my poetry wasn't good enough yet. Thank you for reminding me that I could publish my way. And of course, for the last- minute, final draft review (it's a good thing I have a Grammar Queen like you to help me ☺)

Thank you to Somatic Sorceress, Madelyn, for holding space for me to explore my wild range of expression, giving me a reference point for feeling so deliciously full of self, and asking if *Lover* felt better to me than *Las Vegas Lover* (yes, yes it did).

Thank you to all the creatives at my Open Mic Magic Hour and the poets at The Hub on Canal for witnessing me. For giving me the space to share my poetry and receive your raw, in-the-moment responses to some of the poems in this collection. You inspire me to keep putting myself out there. To keep being brave in love and creativity.

And last, but certainly not least, a special thank you to Angela at the MGM Grand Pool, for being so warm and open when we met. Thank you for our lovely chat about sex, love, and creativity that inspired the poolside poem. I hope you wrote your book (and if you didn't yet, let's make it happen!)

If you're curious about all the Las Vegas places referenced in this collection, here's a complete list:

Harry Reid International Airport

The Las Vegas Strip

Bodies Las Vegas - The Luxor Hotel

Vladimir Kush Fine Art Gallery - Caesar's Palace
Sculptures & escalators - Caesar's Palace

Statue of Liberty - New York-New York

The Mayfair Supper Club – Bellagio Hotel & Casino
Bellagio Art Gallery - Bellagio Hotel & Casino
Bellagio Conservatory & Botanical Gardens, Fountains

LOVE sculpture - The Venetian
Yardbird Table & Bar – The Venetian

Mon Ami Gabi - Paris Las Vegas
Eiffel Tower – Paris Las Vegas

Red Rock Canyon – Mountain Springs, Nevada

Pool - The Signature at MGM Grand
Black jack table - MGM Grand Casino

Gloria Herdt is a writer, poet, and movement artist whose work is deeply rooted in the body and nature. Creativity often wakes her up during the witching hour (and she wouldn't want it any other way). She's passionate about serving artists who desire greater clarity, confidence, and ecstasy in expression.

She lives in New Smyrna Beach, Florida, and loves watching sunrises, eating tacos, trail walking with her rescue dog, and having mind-bending creative conversations with her husband.

Want more of Gloria's creative energy? Subscribe to her *Substack* page or follow her on *Instagram* @gloria.herdt
Want to work with Gloria? Apply at www.gloriaherdt.com

Did you feel something while reading *Lover*?

Leave a review on Amazon + DM me on Instagram.
I'd love to hear from you ☺

@GLORIA.HERDT

Want to write the book that's on your heart?
(maybe even share it with the world …)

Let's connect!
Message me on Instagram or my website
www.gloriaherdt.com

www.ingramcontent.com/pod-product-compliance
Lightning Source LLC
LaVergne TN
LVHW041628070526
838199LV00052B/3279